Unique Adult Career Guide 2016

Dawn Lucan

# Introduction

I still remember my high school days three decades later. I remember the pressure to find the perfect career and college to attend. My high school advisor and teachers was there for me when I needed help with completing college applications. However, I was on my own when it came to deciding upon my future career.

I had some interesting challenges along the way when it came to my career since I have a disability. It made some interesting challenges when it came to dealing with some of my disability characteristics and my chosen career. However, I discovered a way to match my interests and abilities along the way.

If your chosen career requires a college degree or technical training, there is help for you out there. There is financial aid available from the government besides college scholarships. Also, the college offers a disabled students office which offers a variety of adaptations for you to be able to attend school.

The amount of resources has improved since I graduated from high school for high school students. However, it can still be a tricky matter for unique learners. I have included some of my favorite resources to help you with your new journey in life. I have created this career guide to help you find some interesting matches to your interests.

In this book, I often recommend for training after high school your local community college for associate's degree programs. I mention this, so you do not end up with a lot of debt that you could get from a private technical school or college.

I have included in this book a variety of different website resources to help you get started in your chosen career. They include how to write a resume besides some fantastic job search engines that I trust.

*Dawn Lucan*

## Bookkeeper

If you love mathematics or working with numbers, you might be interested in becoming a bookkeeper. You would be most likely working for a small business. You would be keeping track most likely through a computer software program transaction, deposits, or number information. To enter this career field, you need at least a certificate or associate's degree from your local community college.

## Call Center Representative

If you love talking on the telephone and helping people, you might want to become a call center representative. To enter this career field, you need a high school diploma.

## Certified Nursing Assistant

If you love helping people, you might want to become a certified nursing assistant. You could be working in a nursing home, adult day care, or hospital settings. You could be helping the individual with daily life activities and lifting patients. To enter into this career field, you need to be trained for it through your local community college or hospital.

## Chef

If you love to cook for yourself and others, you might want to consider becoming a chef. You could work in a restaurant, hospital, nursing home, diner, etc. Most advanced positions require college training that you can receive at your local community college.

## Computer Technician

If you love to repair things besides working on computers, you might want to consider becoming a computer technician. You could be helping people with their computers with various software and hardware issues. Most of these jobs require an associate's degree from a community college or a bachelor's degree from a college or university depending on the type of position you are looking for.

Customer Service Representative

If you love helping people and problem solve, you would love to become a customer service representative. You could be helping a person over the telephone or in person at a store or business. You would need a high school diploma to enter into this field.

## Food Stager or Food Stylist

If you love taking pictures and cooking, you might want to become a food stager. You could cook the food to the right presentation point, stage it on a plate, and photograph it. You could be working for a publication, television, or large company.

## Graphic Designer

If you love doing a combination of drawing and writing, you might enjoy becoming a graphic artist. You could be working on websites, company logos, print advertisements, posters, various publications, and more. Depending on the employer, you will need at least an associate's degree from a community college to enter into this career field.

## Hair Stylist

If you love working with hair and a creative person, you might want to work as a hair stylist. You could be working in a hair salon or even a movie set. To enter into this career field, you need to have a cosmetology license from your state and have graduated from a beauty/cosmetology school.

## Help Desk Specialist

If you love computers and problem solving, you might want to become a help desk specialist. You could be providing technical support over the telephone for people with software and hardware problems with their computer. To enter into this career field, you should have some background in computers or at least a certificate of completion from your local community college.

## Home Health Aide

If you love helping people and want to work with people with medical problems, you might want to become a home health aide. You could be helping them around the house to various personal care. You need at least a high school diploma to enter into this career field.

## Landscaper

If you love working outside and love plants, you might want to become a landscaper. You could be mowing the lawn, raking leaves, digging holes, trimming plants, and planting flowers, trees or bushes. These jobs are typically done at homes, businesses, and apartment complexes. I must warn you that in most parts of the country that this is a seasonal job. You need a high school diploma to start in this career field.

## Machinist

If you enjoy working with machines or making parts, you might want to become a machinist. You need at least a high school diploma to enter into this career field besides some vocational training through your local four year apprenticeship program, community college, or vocational school.

## Marketing Assistant

If you love being creative and promote a cause or project, you might be interested in becoming a marketing assistant. You need strong interpersonal and communication skills in this field. To enter into this career field, you need at least an associate's degree from your local community college or a bachelor's degree for some positions.

## Mechanic

If you love cars (or trucks) along with problem solving and fixing things, you might want to become a mechanic. You could work for a car (or truck) dealer, repair shop, or service station. To enter into this career field, you need to graduate from a technical (vocational) school or your community college degree along with certification.

## Medical Assistant

If you love helping people and want to work in a physician's office, you might want to become a medical assistant. You could be helping in the office performing administrative duties to taking a patient's medical history. To enter into this career field, you need at least a certificate or associate degree from your community college besides certification.

## Office Manager

If you like working in an office setting doing a variety of different tasks, you might consider becoming an office manager. You could be working for a company in a variety of different industries. You could be handling mail, working on the computer, handling employees, and more depending on the company. To enter into this career field, you need at least an associate's degree from a community college to attend.

## Pastry Chef

If you love to bake, you might want to become a pastry chef. You could be working at a restaurant. You could be baking cakes, pies, cookies, and more. To start in this career, you would need a high school diploma, but some businesses might want at least a certificate of completion from your local community college.

## Pharmacy Technician

If you love handling prescriptions, you might enjoy becoming a pharmacy technician. You could be processing prescriptions under a pharmacist, working with physician offices, and handling payments from customers. You could be working in retail pharmacy stores and hospitals. To enter into this career field, you would need in most places certification which you could find through your local community college.

## Photographer

If you love taking pictures with a camera, you might want to become a photographer. You could work directly for a company or do freelance work. Some even start their own business based on their own interests. For some parts of the career field, you need at least an associate's degree in photography from your local community college. If you go into freelance work or want to own your own business, you might want to take some business courses.

## Prep Cook

If you love to cook, you might want to become a prep cook. You could be working in a restaurant, hospital, or nursing home. You would be preparing vegetables, fruits, and various other foods for food preparation or cooking in the future. To enter this career field, you do not require any formal culinary training for most workplaces.

## Product Demonstrator

If you love showing how products work and talking about them, you could become a product demonstrator. You could work in a grocery store with food or any other retail store. This is mostly part-time work, and you need a high school diploma to start in this career field.

## Property Manager

If you love helping people living in a community, you might enjoy becoming a property manager. You could be working in rental community featuring apartments or townhouses. You could even manage an office building. Responsibilities include marketing, completing various paperwork, supervising repair workers, staff, answering the telephone, and more. To enter this career field, most employers prefer you to have at least a college degree from your local community college.

## Receptionist

If you love greeting and helping people, you would love becoming a receptionist. Besides greeting people, you would be answering the telephone and possibly some form of office work. For some positions, you might only need a high school diploma, but you could for other places need a certificate in business or office work for more advanced workplaces.

## Recreation Assistant

If you love to organize and promote activities for a facility, you would love to become a recreation assistant. You could work in a nursing home, hospital, or consumer agency. To enter into this career field, you need a high school diploma to start.

## Recruiter

If you like meeting people and finding the right person for the job, you might want to become a recruiter. You can specialize in a variety of different fields based on your interests. To enter into this career field, most businesses prefer you to have a bachelor's degree and some experience in human resource field.

## Security Guard

If you love helping people and monitoring situations, you might want to become a security guard. In addition, you need good communication skills and ability to handle a variety of different situations. You could have a job working for a business, hospital, educational institutions, retail stores, or even the government.

## Social Worker

If you love working with people and helping them, you might be interested in becoming a social worker. You could work in a variety of different settings such as a nursing home, hospital, government agency, and a nonprofit organization. You could be working with patients, families, and communities. To enter into this career, you need at least a bachelor's degree in social work from a college or university along with a state license with some businesses.

## Tour Guide

If you have a strong interest in something and expert knowledge of your area, you might want to consider becoming a tour guide. It is a person who leads a group of individuals to various sites in your area based on a theme that you have created. Most of these jobs can be located through the various bus, cruise lines, and tour companies.

## Video Game Designer

If you love playing computer games along with telling a story and computer programming, you would enjoy becoming a video game designer. You would need a minimum of an associate's degree in software design, animation, or computer graphics from your local community college.

## Video Game Tester

If you love video games and write well, you could become a video game tester. You would be playing a video game, look for problems in the video game, and then report in detail the problems to the company. To enter into this career field, you only need a high school diploma, but you need a college degree to advance in this career field.

# Resources

www.careerbuilder.com
www.careeronespot.org
www.careerperfect.com
www.dawn.lucan.com
www.dice.com
www.diversityjobs.com
www.freelancer.com
www.indeed.com
www.monster.com
www.myfuture.com
www.ncil.org
www.nerdwallet.com
www.payscale.com
www.recruitmentqueen.com
www.snagajob.com
www.toptal.com
www.upwork.com